CHRIST'S CARE FOR HIS CHURCHES

A Pastoral Exposition of Revelation 1:9–20

RICHARD CALDWELL

Christ's Care for His Churches: A Pastoral Exposition of Revelation 1:9–20

Copyright © 2025 Richard Caldwell

All rights reserved.

Published by: Kress Biblical Resources

www.kressbiblical.com

Unless otherwise noted, all Scripture references are taken from
The World English Bible, Public Domain
(*"tribulation" has been substituted for "oppression" in Rev. 1:9)

Scripture quotations marked "NASB" are taken from the
(NASB®) New American Standard Bible®, Copyright © 1960,
1971, 1977, 1995, 2020 by The Lockman Foundation. Used by permission. All rights reserved. www.Lockman.org

ISBN: 978-1-934952-88-7

CONTENTS

Divine Comfort for Fellow Partakers 5

Divine Comfort in Suffering 11

Divine Comfort in Scripture 17

Divine Comfort in Our Savior 21

Divine Comfort in Security 29

Divine Comfort and Courage 35

1

DIVINE COMFORT FOR FELLOW PARTAKERS

Revelation 1:9–20

I John, your brother and partner with you in the tribulation*, kingdom, and perseverance in Christ Jesus, was on the isle that is called Patmos because of God's Word and the testimony of Jesus Christ. ¹⁰ I was in the Spirit on the Lord's Day, and I heard behind me a loud voice, like a trumpet ¹¹ saying, "What you see, write in a book and send to the seven assemblies: to Ephesus, Smyrna, Pergamum, Thyatira, Sardis, Philadelphia, and to Laodicea."

¹² I turned to see the voice that spoke with me. Having turned, I saw seven golden lamp stands. ¹³ And among the lamp stands was one like a son of man, clothed with a robe reaching down to his feet, and with a golden sash around his chest. ¹⁴ His head and his hair were white as white wool, like snow. His eyes were like a flame of fire. ¹⁵ His feet were like burnished brass, as if it had been refined in a furnace. His voice was like the voice of many waters. ¹⁶ He had seven stars in his right hand. Out of his mouth proceeded a sharp two-edged sword. His face was like the sun shining at its brightest. ⁱ⁷ When I saw him, I fell at his feet like a dead man.

He laid his right hand on me, saying, "Don't be afraid. I am the first and the last, ¹⁸ and the Living one. I was dead, and behold, I am alive forever and ever. Amen. I have the keys of Death and of Hades. ¹⁹ Write therefore the things which you have seen, and the things which are, and the things which will happen hereafter. ²⁰ The mystery of the seven stars which you saw in my right hand, and the seven golden lamp stands is this: The seven stars are the angels of the seven assemblies. The seven lamp stands are seven assemblies."

A Timeless … and a Timely Message

The book of Revelation has a timeless purpose. Here we are, roughly 2,000 years after it was written, and this is the Lord's Word to us as His church. But we need to remember that it not only has a timeless purpose; when it was first given, it had a *timely* purpose. In fact, this timely purpose—in principle and application—serves a timeless purpose.

We benefit today in the same way that the seven churches mentioned in our text benefited on the day they first received the letter. When the book of Revelation was communicated to the Apostle John and then given to the churches, the infant church was a suffering church.

John himself was suffering. He was living on a small island off the coast of Asia Minor called Patmos—a prison island where the Romans banished their political opponents. Tradition holds that he was forced into a prison labor camp while on that island. John was there not as a criminal, but because of his Christian faith; he tells us he is there *"because of God's Word and the testimony of Jesus"* (1:9).

Believers were suffering, and John himself exemplified that suffering. There was more difficulty on the horizon, which is why, as the Lord Jesus communicates with these churches, He acknowledges their suffering, praises their endurance, and exhorts them to continue in their endurance.

For example, in Christ's message to Pergamum in Revelation 2:13, the Lord says, *"I know your works and where you dwell, where Satan's throne is. You hold firmly to my name, and didn't deny my faith in the days of Antipas my witness, my faithful one, who was killed among you, where Satan dwells."* This was not just mild suffering; some of these churches had experienced the tragedy of martyrdom. John himself knew the pain of losing his brother James through martyrdom (Acts 12:2). Yet even amid such trials, the Lord Jesus affirms the difficulty of their circumstances, recognizes their faithfulness, and commends them for remaining steadfast.

Divine Care for Suffering Churches

I want us to recognize that the book of Revelation is a care package for suffering churches. It served the suffering churches of its time and continues to serve suffering churches throughout history. It reminds us of the ultimate victory of Jesus, our security in Christ, and the way He cares for us. It offers a prophetic, panoramic view of the rest of time stretching into eternity that assures us of God's sovereignty and our safety in Him.

The Revealer ... and the One Revealed

The primary way that God comforts us through this book is in the revelation of Christ Himself. The Father gives the message to the Son, who gives it to an angel, who gives it to John, who gives it to the churches. In this process, Christ serves as both the Revealer and the One being revealed. This is communicated by the One who had died and is now alive, clearly indicating it is Jesus that John witnesses.

In Revelation 1:17–18, John writes, *"When I saw him, I fell at his feet like a dead man. He laid his right hand on me, saying, 'Don't be afraid. I am the first and the last, ^{18} and the Living one. I was dead, and behold, I am alive forever and ever. Amen. I have the keys of Death and of Hades."* This is Jesus speaking to John and addressing the churches. He knows His church, and as we will see, He is present with His church and communicates directly to it.

This is our Lord communicating to us. As He begins to give this message to John, He expresses what all His people share in common. At the very start of the book, our Lord reveals what belongs to our fellowship as believers, offering comfort and confidence to His suffering people.

We will focus on Christ's comfort to His hurting people through the knowledge of what we share in common. I recognize that every day brings a variety of experiences to any given believer. I have no doubt that someone reading this is going through an especially difficult, perhaps fearful or threatening time. While I may not know the specifics of your struggles due to your faith in Christ, my prayer for you is that you find comfort in the words of your Savior and in the reminder of Who and what you belong to.

In Revelation 1:9–20, we see four glorious realities in the chapters that follow—four gifts of comfort to believers—that we all share together because we know Jesus.

2

DIVINE COMFORT IN SUFFERING

Revelation 1:9

I John, your brother and partner with you in the tribulation*, kingdom, and perseverance in Christ Jesus, was on the isle that is called Patmos because of God's Word and the testimony of Jesus Christ.

Fellow Partakers of a Most Precious Title

A Title of Humility

Notice how John describes himself. In verses 1 and 2, he has already said he is a slave of God and a slave of Christ. Then, in verse 4, he introduces himself again: *"John, to the seven assemblies that are in Asia."*

John simply writes as one who is in fellowship with the Lord and is therefore able to give voice to what he has received and continues to receive from the Lord—and what we all receive from the Lord: grace and peace.

A Title of Highest Honor

In verse 9, John introduces himself as *"your brother and partner with you in the tribulation*, kingdom, and perseverance in*

Christ Jesus." Here we see John's humility. He could have presented himself as an apostle or as an elder, as he does in some of his letters. He might have highlighted his roles as a preacher or a teacher, but instead, he chooses the most fundamental and precious title: "brother."

As believers, we have all been taken out of the world of lost humanity and transferred into the kingdom of God's Son (Col. 1:13). We are now children of the living God, and through new birth, regeneration, adoption, and justification by faith alone in Christ alone, we have become family. This is why John opens by saying he is *"your brother."* If you are truly a believer, John's self-designation here indicates what will always be the most cherished title you possess. It doesn't matter what you accomplish in the name of the Lord or how others may recognize your work; the most precious title for you is "child of God," and in relation to other believers, "your brother or sister in Christ."

What an amazing truth that God has loved us in this way—making us His children, forgiving us all our sins, and making us a part of His family forever. This is what we celebrate. This is our glory. This is our boasting—that *we belong to Christ.*

Fellow Partakers in Affliction

Shared Hardship

John's humility is further revealed in how he identifies not only as our brother but also as our companion in suffering. *"I John, your brother and partner"* he writes, expressing fellowship with us as brothers and sisters *"in the* *tribulation*, kingdom, and perseverance in Christ Jesus, was on the isle that is called Patmos because of God's Word and the testimony of Jesus Christ."* Yet, he does not see himself as alone in his suffering. He calls himself a partner or a fellow partaker in these experiences, emphasizing that this suffering is a shared reality among all believers. It is a suffering unique only to believers, but not unique in that all believers partake of suffering for Christ.

He reminds the churches that they are in this together. We all share together in the tribulation and kingdom and perseverance—each of which is found in Jesus. While these experiences are uniquely Christian, they are not exclusive to just one or a few individuals; they are experienced, to some extent, by all of us.

Shared Responsibility to Persevere

The singular article preceding the three nouns (*the* tribulation and kingdom and perseverance) suggests that they should be considered together. Each word highlights something unique, yet collectively they convey one idea: affliction. The two terms "kingdom" and "perseverance" connect this oppression or tribulation as being not what the world experiences, but what is particularly connected to Christ's kingdom. And as such, it requires endurance and patience as we await it.[1]

We understand the challenges faced by those who are part of Christ's kingdom spiritually yet are still waiting for the kingdom He will establish upon His return from heaven to earth. This means that our suffering, as we

---

[1] See Robert L. Thomas, *Revelation 1–7: An Exegetical Commentary* (Chicago: Moody Publishers, 1992), 86.

await that kingdom, demands patience and endurance. This trouble, tribulation, affliction is specifically linked to the kingdom and requires perseverance. That is why perseverance or patience is consistently emphasized in the messages to the seven churches. For instance, in Revelation 2:2, the church at Ephesus is commended for its works, toil, and patient endurance, as well as its ability to reject false apostles. The Lord acknowledges their ongoing patience and endurance for His name's sake, noting they have not grown weary.

Shared Hope

What does our Lord mean when He speaks of suffering and enduring patiently? It involves not only patience in the moment but also patience in light of eternity. There is another day coming; circumstances will not remain as they are now. Our suffering will come to an end, leading to victory. Thus, we are called to live in and through our troubles with faith, looking to the end of the journey, looking to the triumph of Christ. This vision provides us with the courage and strength to endure, even in the face of severe suffering—including martyrdom if necessary. We must honor the Lord with faithfulness until the day when we see our Savior face to face.

The church at Thyatira is recognized for its works, love, faith, service, and patient endurance, with its latter works surpassing the first (Rev. 2:19). Similarly, the church at Philadelphia is praised in Revelation 3:10 for keeping the word about patient endurance, and as a result, they will be kept from the coming hour of trial that will affect the entire world.

John, who humbly identifies himself as a brother, recognizes that this suffering is a shared experience within the church. All believers are called to endure trouble as we patiently wait for the kingdom—our shared hope.

Steadfastness Required

This aligns with the general instruction given to churches wherever Paul ministered. When new believers came to faith in Christ and churches were formed, one of the first teachings emphasized was the necessity of patient endurance—steadfastness in hope.

In Acts 14:21–22, after preaching the gospel and making many disciples, Paul and his companions returned to Lystra, Iconium, and Antioch to strengthen the disciples, encouraging them to continue in the faith by reminding them that *"through many afflictions we must enter into God's Kingdom."* These believers are already in the kingdom in a spiritual sense, yet Paul emphasizes that tribulations are a part of entering the kingdom of God.

At the end of the journey, when the kingdom is ushered in, those who will enter are the people who have endured the many trials that belong to the Christian life. This is the kind of patience our Lord speaks of through John.

The first comforting truth we share is the knowledge that we are called to suffer: *"Yes, all who desire to live godly in Christ Jesus will suffer persecution"* (2 Tim. 3:12). This is something that belongs to all the people; we share in this unique kind of suffering—Christian suffering—where we encounter the world's wrath, stemming from its hatred for God and His Word.

Each of us will face this challenge at some point during our Christian journey, and we must learn to endure it patiently. God's people share a fellowship in suffering.

3

DIVINE COMFORT IN SCRIPTURE

Revelation 1:10–11

I was in the Spirit on the Lord's Day, and I heard behind me a loud voice, like a trumpet [11] *saying, "What you see, write in a book and send to the seven assemblies: to Ephesus, Smyrna, Pergamum, Thyatira, Sardis, Philadelphia, and to Laodicea."*

The Believer's Care Package from God

In Revelation 1:10, John hears a voice, which we recognize as the voice of the glorified Christ, instructing John to write down his vision. By doing so, the Lord is providing His churches with His inscripturated words.

John's being "*in the Spirit*" on the Lord's Day speaks of a special state of spiritual awareness—a God-given condition of mind and body that prepares him to receive this unique form of divine communication. While the writers of Scripture often expressed their own thoughts and words, they were guided by the Spirit of God, ensuring that what they wrote perfectly reflected God's own thoughts and words. This process allowed them to write His Word without error (2 Tim. 3:16).

However, there were times when God imparted New Covenant revelation to the Apostles for the infant church, and these revelations came in the state that John refers to as being "*in the Spirit.*" This state is a God-produced spiritual condition in which he received these visions from the Lord. This experience was unique to the Apostles, unique to the apostolic era. God is not giving any new revelation today. No one in our day will ever experience being "*in the Spirit*" in the same way John did.

A Shared Vision

John's vision of the glorified Christ is not meant solely for him; it is intended for the churches. This signifies that Jesus is providing truth to John in a visual manner for the benefit of the churches, which was to be inscripturated. What we have in this book of the Bible is the result of what John saw. We have it as one of the 66 inspired books that represent our living God communicating to His people. Thus, it is in essence a divine care package for His suffering churches.

These seven real assemblies in Asia Minor are about to receive what Jesus revealed to John, written down so they can read it and hear it. They do not witness the vision themselves; they read and hear what John saw. Today, we also read and hear what John experienced, which unites the people of God as recipients of His truth through His Word.

While God's Word is given to the world in terms of responsibility, accountability, and evangelism, it is specifically the people who actually receive this Word with believing hearts, those with ears ready to hear and hearts of flesh instead of stone, who truly grasp the revelation that God has provided. These are the redeemed, who come to know this revelation through the knowledge given to them. God sent His Word to us, working through His Spirit so that we could hear, see, repent, and believe, ultimately trusting in Christ as our Lord and Savior. This book now belongs to us, His people.

The Believer's Care Package is Delivered Exclusively to the Church

Beware of anyone who claims to be a Christian but has no regard for the Lord's church. Such a claim does not accord with Christ. Here, Jesus instructs John to write this down on a scroll to be sent to seven real churches in his time: Ephesus, Smyrna, Pergamum, Thyatira, Sardis, Philadelphia, and Laodicea.

Before the printing press and widespread Bible distribution, hearing what was written in the scroll required being part of the church. If you weren't among the gathered in Ephesus, in Smyrna, in Pergamum, in Thyatira, in Sardis, in Philadelphia, in Laodicea, you would miss the message.

In Revelation, the Lord of glory reveals how God will conclude all things and what the end of the story will be. Notably, He does not send this glorious message to the White House or news stations, so to speak; He sends it to His church. Jesus Himself said, *"I will build my church"*

(Matt. 16:18). And if you love Jesus, you must also love His church. Indeed, one cannot truly love the Lord Jesus without also loving His bride, the church. Our Lord gives His church the opportunity to receive His Word, which is what we all share in common: the Scriptures.

Are you a part of the people of The Book? Is the Word of God nourishment for your soul? Does it light your path, provide confidence for your heart, comfort for your hurts, and cleanse your life to produce in you what pleases God? Do you delight in it and take joy in it? Read Psalm 19 or Psalm 119 and listen as the Word of God is praised because God Himself is praised. Reflect on whether that is your attitude toward the Scriptures. This is what saved people share: we are the people of The Book.

We have suffering in common, and we have the Scriptures in common—Scriptures given to address our needs amid suffering. This is the purpose of the Lord's message to these suffering churches. Why is John on this island? Because of the Word of God and the witness of Jesus. Thus, our suffering is connected to the Scriptures. But the Scripture—the Word of God—is the source of comfort in our suffering, because the Scriptures reveal the Person and work of Jesus Christ.

Therefore, in the next chapter we will see that God's people share fellowship in our glorious Shepherd—our sovereign Savior.

4

DIVINE COMFORT IN OUR SAVIOR

Revelation 1:12–18

I turned to see the voice that spoke with me. Having turned, I saw seven golden lamp stands. [13] And among the lamp stands was one like a son of man, clothed with a robe reaching down to his feet, and with a golden sash around his chest. [14] His head and his hair were white as white wool, like snow. His eyes were like a flame of fire. [15] His feet were like burnished brass, as if it had been refined in a furnace. His voice was like the voice of many waters. [16] He had seven stars in his right hand. Out of his mouth proceeded a sharp two-edged sword. His face was like the sun shining at its brightest.

[17] When I saw him, I fell at his feet like a dead man.

He laid his right hand on me, saying, "Don't be afraid. I am the first and the last, [18] and the Living one. I was dead, and behold, I am alive forever and ever. Amen. I have the keys of Death and of Hades."

Fellow Partakers in the Shepherd-Savior

In these verses, John is seeing the glorified Christ. As we reflect on what he saw and the symbols he described, we are reminded of the One who has taken hold of our lives. He has you, and you have Him.

His Humanity and Messianic Identity

In Revelation 1:12–18 we see Christ's humanity and His messianic identity; He is referred to as Son of Man. John states in verses 12–13, "*I turned to see the voice that spoke with me. Having turned, I saw seven golden lamp stands. And among the lamp stands was one like a son of man.*" This echoes Daniel 7:13, where the Messiah is described as One "*like a son of man.*" This title was one of Jesus' favorite self-designations during His time on earth, emphasizing the reality that He took to Himself an additional nature in order to save us.

What did our Lord do to be our Shepherd and Savior forever? He saved us from our sins, addressing our greatest need: forgiveness for our guilt before God. This forgiveness cannot be achieved through our own works but only through the work that Jesus accomplished. The eternal Son of God stepped out of heaven and took to Himself a sinless human nature through the virgin conception and birth.

He is forever God, but at a specific point in history, He became a man. The God-man, the Son of Man, walked the earth, lived a sinless life, died on the cross as our substitute, and was raised from the dead bodily. As He says of Himself here, "*I was dead, and behold, I am alive.*" He conquered death and the grave, ascended into heaven, and is coming again. This is the One for whom we wait, as described by John—"*one like a son of man.*" This is the God-man, the Messiah, who has been given the title and deed to the kingdom of God (Dan. 7:13–14).

His Royalty and Majesty

In John's vision, Christ is clothed in a robe reaching to His feet and girded with a golden sash. Some argue that this attire signifies royalty, while others claim it indicates priesthood. Our Lord is both King and Priest. He is our great High Priest and He is the King of Kings and Lord of Lords (Heb. 3:1; Rev. 17:14). Therefore, I will not debate for one over the other. I simply affirm, "Yes and amen."

He is the King and the great High Priest, and the very way He appears communicates royalty and majesty.

His Divine Wisdom and Dignity

Christ's appearance also conveys wisdom and dignity. His head and hair, as described in verse 14, were white like wool, like snow. In Daniel 7, a similar description—the Ancient of Days—is given to God the Father. This points to the deity of Christ, as well as His wisdom and His dignity. In Daniel 7:9, it says, "*I watched until thrones were placed, and one who was Ancient of Days sat. His clothing was white as snow, and the hair of his head like pure wool. His throne was fiery flames, and its wheels burning fire.*"

Revelation 1 reveals Jesus of Nazareth, who died, was raised, ascended, and is glorified. His head and His hair are white like white wool, like snow. Proverbs 16:31 and

20:29 speak of gray hair in general as proverbial of dignity—wisdom and honor, and even a righteous life. John's description of Jesus' white hair is superlative, which is indicative of our risen Savior's perfect and infinite wisdom, dignity, honor, and righteousness.

His Holiness and Omniscience

As God's throne in Daniel 7 was ablaze with fire, signifying God's holiness, so here Christ's eyes being like a flame of fire reflect Christ's holiness. Moreover, this indicates that He does not judge by appearance; He judges with righteous judgment. His omniscience sees to the very core of what is true and real. His eyes burn through the dross of what we would pretend. He knows all. He sees all. He is sovereign over all.

Furthermore, mere humans take in light through our eyes. The God-man not only sees with perfect vision that penetrates to the very soul, He also is the source of light, holiness, and truth as His eyes project divine light on all in His view.

His Omnipotence and Authority

Our Shepherd possesses the strength and authority of God Himself. In Revelation 1:15, His feet are not made of clay, but rather burnished brass or bronze, "*as if it had been refined in a furnace. His voice was like the voice of many waters*"—symbolizing strength and authority, deserving reverence due the One destined to judge one day.

The altar upon which burnt offerings were offered, made of bronze, may also be wrapped up in this symbolism, as He is the judge who gave His life for sins. He will judge those who have not trusted in Him and His payment for their sins.

But to those who put their trust solely in Him and His finished work, Jesus' feet here are beautiful and His voice pure joy. Indeed, "*How beautiful on the mountains are the feet of him who brings good news, who publishes peace, who brings good news, who proclaims salvation, who says to Zion, 'Your God reigns!'*" (Isa. 52:7 used by way of illustration).

Christ's Threefold Kindness and Care for His People

What is most prominent in this vision is the imagery that conveys His care for His people. The One just described is the One who cares for us. He is the One who cares for His church. In verse 16, it says He holds seven stars in His right hand. These stars represent the angels or messengers to the seven churches, proclaimers of God's truth (cf. v. 20). He stands in the midst of seven golden lampstands. Our Lord stands with and among His people. A sharp two-edged sword comes out of His mouth. Christ's Word—the very Word of God—purifies, protects, and preserves His church, because He is the truth. And His face shines like the sun in its power.

This serves as a reminder, *first*, that the blessings we receive from our Lord are *personal*. They come from His very being—His own Person. We often mistakenly think of God's blessings as separate from Him, as if He gives them without involving Himself.

We need to remember that every blessing we receive, even the material gifts from His hand, expresses His character and nature. His unchanging, always-faithful, trustworthy nature, as well as His goodness, holiness, kindness, grace, and mercy, are on display in each good gift.

Second, our Shepherd shines with divine holiness, yet is sufficient to save. Note the following sample verses:

> *Turn us again, God. Cause your face to shine, and we will be saved ... Turn us again, God of Armies. Cause your face to shine, and we will be saved ... Turn us again, Yahweh God of Armies. Cause your face to shine, and we will be saved.* (Ps. 80:3, 7, 19)
>
> *Yahweh spoke to Moses, saying, "Speak to Aaron and to his sons, saying, 'This is how you shall bless the children of Israel.' You shall tell them, 'Yahweh bless you, and keep you. Yahweh make his face to shine on you, and be gracious to you. Yahweh lift up his face toward you, and give you peace.'"* (Num. 6:22–26)

The blessing in Numbers 6 is a common prayer that the Lord's face would shine upon His people, reflecting His divine presence, with blessing emanating from His Person. Psalm 80 and Numbers 6 beautifully confirm that salvation, protection, blessing, and peace radiate from the face of God. And we rejoice that in God's sovereign grace, there is a sense in which we too have seen His face. As Paul says in 2 Corinthians 4:6, *"it is God who said, 'Light will shine out of darkness,' who has shone in our hearts to give the light of the knowledge of the glory of God in the face of Jesus Christ."*

John describes the Lord Jesus, standing with His face shining in full radiance, reminding us of His holiness. We cannot approach Him apart from God's grace, which underscores the nature of all that we receive. Everything comes from Him and through Him, as holiness and grace shine forth from the Savior.

Third, our Shepherd Himself—His very Person—is our greatest comfort. This revelation begins with a vision of Jesus Himself because Christ is both the revealer and the primary subject of this revelation. Recognizing this brings forth a profound lesson: in times of suffering, Christ offers comfort to His churches, starting with a reminder of who He is.

The greatest comfort God provides in any situation is Himself. Wherever we are, He is with us. Whatever we endure, He is there—not only aware of our struggles but also caring for us and controlling our circumstances. "*And we know God causes all things to work together for good, for those who love God and are called according to His purpose*" (Rom. 8:28). You can trust that. John MacArthur comments,

> John's readers took comfort in the knowledge that Christ will one day return in glory and defeat His enemies. The description of those momentous events takes up most of the book of Revelation, but the vision of Jesus Christ that begins the book does not describe Jesus in His future glory, but depicts Him in the present as the glorified Lord of the church. In spite of all the disappointments, the Lord had not abandoned His church or His promises. This powerful vision of Christ's present ministry to them must have provided

great hope and comfort to the wondering and suffering churches to whom John wrote.[2]

His Blessings are Shared by All Believers—Suffering, the Scriptures, the Savior, and Security

What do we share as believers? We share in the privilege of *suffering* together for Christ as we anticipate His coming kingdom.

We share in the glorious gift of the *Scriptures*—given by God to fortify our faith until we see our Savior face to face.

We share in the Person of the *Savior* Himself, who intercedes for us in heaven, cares for us, and communicates to us. He is all we need, and is *the* all-in-all for us until we are ushered into His very presence.

---

[2] John MacArthur, *Revelation 1–11*, The MacArthur New Testament Commentary. Accordance electronic ed. (Chicago: Moody Press, 1999), 52.

5

DIVINE COMFORT IN SECURITY

Revelation 1:17–20

When I saw him, I fell at his feet like a dead man. He laid his right hand on me, saying, "Don't be afraid. I am the first and the last, [18] and the Living one. I was dead, and behold, I am alive forever and ever. Amen. I have the keys of Death and of Hades. [19] Write therefore the things which you have seen, and the things which are, and the things which will happen hereafter. [20] The mystery of the seven stars which you saw in my right hand, and the seven golden lamp stands is this: The seven stars are the angels of the seven assemblies. The seven lamp stands are seven assemblies."

In our final verses, we see how we share in divine security. Because of the grace of God and his saving power, we are safe from enemies or circumstances, past or present, as we entrust ourselves to our faithful Shepherd.

Fellow Partakers in Security

He is Our Kind Shepherd

We have no reason to fear. Why? Because our Shepherd is a kind Shepherd as He deals with John, who represents all of us in our weakness. Even though he is saved and redeemed, John falls at the feet of Jesus as if he were dead. Yet our Lord not only raises him up, but He also places His right hand on John. He doesn't just raise him up. He says these glorious words: "*Don't be afraid.*"

Aren't you grateful to experience the kindness of your Lord every day? He is not someone who saves us and then frowns upon us throughout our lives. Spoiler alert: He knew what He was getting when He saved you. He knew your strengths after conversion and was aware of all your weaknesses. He already knew the triumphs He would produce in your life, and He knew already what failures you would produce in your life. He paid for all of your sins, all of them—every single one—with His blood. He has brought you to Himself not based on your performance, but because He has performed everything necessary so that you will never be lost again (cf. Rev. 1:5–6). He is our kind Shepherd.

He is Our Conquering Shepherd

When you recognize His holiness and your own smallness, His kindness reassures you: "*Don't be afraid.*" He can say this because he is divine: "*Do not fear.*" Don't you know, John, the One who has loved you? Don't you know the One who has saved you? Don't you know the

One who has control over your life and all of the churches?

Jesus says, "*I am the first and the last ... I was dead, and behold, I am alive forever and ever.*" He states this speaking of His resurrection, but before that, in verse 18, He calls Himself *the Living One*. He preceded it all—He's the first. He follows it all—He's the last. That is, He is eternal in His divine nature. Uncreated, He has always existed as the eternal Son of God, possessing life within Himself.

We, on the other hand, are creatures who receive life from the hand of God. God received life from no one. God does not exist because someone made Him live; He has always existed, and He gives life. Jesus *is Himself* eternal life.

Through the incarnation, Christ becomes a conquering Shepherd-Savior. He states in verse 18, "*I was dead.*" How does the forever-existent one become dead? The answer lies in the incarnation. He was dead in the sense of His human nature, not in His divine nature. But behold, He declares, "*I am alive forever and ever ... I have the keys of Death and of Hades.*" He is always sovereign over death and Hades in His divine nature, but now, as our Redeemer, He has authority over death and the grave.

We have nothing to fear—not even in death. We have nothing to fear—not even in the grave—because the Lord of death and the grave is also the Lord of life—and Lord of *our* lives. He has taken hold of us, never to let us go. As He is alive forever and ever, He promises resurrection for all His people. We, too, will be alive forever and ever.

He is Our Purposeful Shepherd

In verse 19, Jesus told John, "*Write therefore the things which you have seen, and the things which are, and the things which will happen hereafter.*" The Father entrusted Jesus with a message for John, and He is fulfilling that by enlisting John to write. Here our Shepherd-Savior provides an outline for the entire book: "*Write the things which you have seen*" refers to the vision in chapter one. Write "*the things which are*" indicates that John should document the messages for the existing churches, which extends through chapter 3. Finally, write about "*the things which will happen hereafter*" starts in chapter 4 and continues throughout the rest of the book.

Thus, our Lord clearly outlines what we need, what is beneficial for His people, and what He intends for us to understand. I am grateful, as I know you are too, that as believers we live our lives aware that everything comes from the hands of a purposeful Shepherd. There is nothing we face that is without purpose. While we may waste opportunities, our Lord's plans and purposes for us are perfect, and nothing we encounter is accidental.

He is Our Ever-Present Shepherd

He is our kind Shepherd, our divine Shepherd, our conquering and purposeful Shepherd—and gloriously, our ever-present Shepherd. In this vision, our Lord is standing right in the midst of His churches. John turns around and sees Him standing in the middle of the lampstands, which are identified as the seven churches in verse 20. He stands in the midst of Ephesus, Smyrna, Pergamum, Thyatira, Sardis, Philadelphia, and Laodicea.

He is also present with every true church in the world today.

In His hand, He holds both the protection and discipline of the messengers to these churches. I interpret *aggeloi* in verse 20 (translated as either "angels" or "messengers") as messengers, preachers, and teachers. He holds these men, like John, who will suffer for the Word of God and the testimony of Christ. They have nothing to fear because they are in Jesus' right hand. Nothing happens without His permission or His purpose.

In this context, Christ's right hand signifies security, safety, rest, peace, confidence, and joy. Jesus said in John 10:27–28: *"My sheep hear my voice, and I know them, and they follow me. I give eternal life to them. They will never perish, and no one will snatch them out of my hand."* In Revelation 2:1, He says, *"To the angel of the assembly in Ephesus write: 'He who holds the seven stars in his right hand, he who walks among the seven golden lamp stands says these things.'"*

With the very first church, He reminds them, "I am here, and I Myself am your security."

Do we really trust our Shepherd? He is kind, He is conquering, He is purposeful, and He is ever-present.

6

DIVINE COMFORT AND COURAGE

Throughout this book, we have seen four glorious realities in Revelation 1:9–20—four gifts of comfort to believers—that we all share together because we know Jesus.

Comfort in Suffering

First, we have seen how our God comforts His suffering people. He reminds us of what we as believers all share in together. Yes, we share in suffering. Sometimes it is mild, but sometimes it can be serious—martyrdom or imprisonment (as church history can attest to, or even for some in the world today in various countries). Christian suffering is a mark of belonging to Christ and the Christian family. It serves for the glory of God and the good of our souls. We have this in common, and God has provided everything we need to patiently endure it.

Comfort in the Scriptures

Second, we have comfort in the Scriptures together. He has given us His Word. The One communicating the

Word to us in a deeply personal way—blessing emanating from His own being, His face shining upon us—is our Shepherd, our Savior, the Lord Jesus Christ.

No matter what we are going through, we are the most secure and safe people on earth. We know the end. Do you understand this? Are you aware that suffering is part of your fellowship in Christ, or are you surprised by it, as if something strange is happening (1 Pet. 4:12)?

Philippians 3:10 speaks of that which is uniquely Christian suffering, *"that I may know him, and the power of his resurrection, and the fellowship of his sufferings, becoming conformed to his death."* Your suffering is actually on behalf of Jesus Himself. Remember when Jesus said to Saul of Tarsus on the road to Damascus, *"Saul, Saul, why are you persecuting me?"* Who was Saul persecuting? People. But these were people who belonged to Jesus.

As previously mentioned, 2 Timothy 3:12 says, *"Yes, and all who desire to live godly in Christ Jesus will suffer persecution."* However, your persecution will correspond to your representation of Him. Why was John on Patmos? For *the Word of God* and for the *testimony of Jesus*.

I want to exhort you, my brothers and sisters—be faithful with the Word of God. Be courageous with the truth, and you will encounter the kind of suffering that John describes. You will face it simply by being faithful to the Word. Don't play the coward. Do not try to spare yourself when your Lord did not spare Himself but gave Himself for you.

Do you realize He sent His Word to care for you? Do you see His Word in that light? The book of Revelation is Christ's care for you. This is how we endure patiently;

this is how we are sustained—through the living Word of God, which comes out of His mouth like a sharp sword. This is how He meets the needs of His people.

Comfort in the Savior Himself, Who is Our Security

Our *third* comfort is how Christ reveals *Himself.* Do you see it this way? Do you consider Christ to be your treasure? Of all the ways He could have comforted His people, what does He do? He gives us a picture of who His is right now. Whatever you are experiencing, your anchor is Christ. Your joy is Christ. Your comfort is Christ. Your reason for existence is Christ. Do you see it this way?

He is your treasure. What do you need for comfort today? What do you need for encouragement? Just the intimate knowledge that you have Christ. He is your Savior—your all-sufficient Savior.

As thus our *fourth* comfort is connected to this. Because His is your all-sufficient Savior, He is your security. As a result, you know you are safe. Hebrews 7:25 states, *"Therefore He is also able to save forever those who come to God through Him, since He always lives to make intercession for them"* (NASB).

Again, when John begins this letter, it is not the future Jesus coming in glory that he describes, but the present Jesus—our great High Priest in heaven. This means we are safe until we reach the end of our journey.[3]

---

[3] See also John MacArthur, *Revelation 1–11*, The MacArthur New Testament Commentary. Accordance electronic ed. (Chicago: Moody Press, 1999), 52.

Courage to Persevere Until the End

Each of the messages to the seven churches in Revelation 2–3 begins with one of the characteristics of Christ revealed in Revelation 1. And notably, each of the messages to the seven churches in chapters 2 and 3 ends with a promise to the one who overcomes.

Seeing Christ in His present divine splendor through this passage is a vital means by which the Holy Spirit gives His people the courage to overcome and persevere to the end.

Therefore, when you find yourself in the midst of suffering for Christ, remember that this suffering is unique to those who are in the family of God. And let your privileged position as a child of God give you courage to persevere.

As well, in the midst of suffering for your Christian faith, turn to the Scriptures that reveal our great Savior Who is our security and hope. Search them diligently. Delight in them. Take refuge in Christ as He is revealed in them. In Him, through the Scriptures, you will find strength to overcome and persevere.

Remember that your Savior is perfect in wisdom and even now serves as your Mediator in glory. Remember that He sees and knows perfectly your pain, your needs, your shortcomings—and He knows perfectly how He will perfect you and preserve you to the end.

Remember His beautiful feet that reflect the Good News that He Himself is our sacrifice, our righteousness, and our eternal life. And look into His glorious face, shining like the sun—to find blessing and salvation.

Remember His command—"*Don't be afraid.*" Remember His sovereignty over every detail from the first to the last, because He is *the first and the last*. And remember His victory and sovereignty over death and the grave.

Take courage, dear brother and sister. Persevere and praise our Lord and Savior, Jesus Christ. *He is coming soon.*

www.ingramcontent.com/pod-product-compliance
Lightning Source LLC
Chambersburg PA
CBHW070047070426
42449CB00012BA/3174